# Eucharistic
## *Spirituality*

OSCAR LUKEFAHR, C.M.

**Liguori**
ONE LIGUORI DRIVE
LIGUORI MO 63057-9999

Imprimi Potest:
Thomas D. Picton, C.Ss.R.
Provincial, Denver Province
The Redemptorists

Imprimatur:
Most Reverend Robert J. Hermann
Auxiliary Bishop
Archdiocese of St. Louis

Scripture citations are taken from the *New Revised Standard Version of the Bible,* copyright © 1989 by the Division of Christian Education of the National Council of Churches of Christ in the USA. All rights reserved. Used with permission.

Excerpts from the English translation of the *Catechism of the Catholic Church* for the United States of America, copyright © 1994, United States Catholic Conference, Inc.—Libreria Editrice Vaticana; English translation of the *Catechism of the Catholic Church: Modifications from the Editio Typica,* copyright © 1997, United States Catholic Conference, Inc.—Libreria Editrice Vaticana. Used with permission.

This pamphlet is an adaptation of a chapter from *We Worship: A Guide to the Catholic Mass,* Liguori Publications, 2004.

Liguori Publications, a nonprofit corporation, is an apostolate of the Redemptorists. To learn more about the Redemptorists, visit Redemptorists.com.

To order, call 1-800-325-9521
www.liguori.org
Cover image: Gene Plaisted, OSC

# Foreword

She was young, beautiful, a prominent socialite from a prestigious family, a patriot during the Revolutionary War, the mother of five children, a devout Episcopalian, a woman of charm and education—and now, a widow. Her beloved husband, William, had succumbed to tuberculosis on a business cruise with his wife to Livorno, Italy, in 1803. While tending to his burial, she was given hospitality by the Fillichi family. She was very moved by their love for Jesus in the Eucharist. She would often accompany them to Mass; she would marvel as they prepared for holy Communion and was in awe of their reverence. She would make visits to the Blessed Sacrament with them and kneel before the tabernacle.

On the Feast of Corpus Christi, she stood on the corner while the procession with the Eucharist passed by. As all the Italians knelt down in quiet prayer and adoration, she heard another American snidely remark, "These peasants think that bread is really the Son of God!" Deep in her soul, the answer came forth, "So do I!" When she returned to New York, she began instructions in the Catholic faith and, at the cost of much sacrifice, scorn, and loss of family, friends, and wealth, she entered the Church in 1805.

On September 14, 1975, Pope Paul VI canonized her as the first native-born American saint. Her name? Elizabeth Ann Bayley Seton.

That's the awesome power of the Eucharist, my friends. That's the draw, the magnetism, of the Blessed Sacrament.

The Eucharist is "the mystery of faith," which we can never fully comprehend. But that does not mean we should not study this mystery, read about it, meditate on it, and pray often before it and about it.

Remember what Pope Saint Pius X taught: "This side of paradise, there is no better way to be united to Jesus than by worthily receiving Him in Holy Communion."

*O sacrament most holy,*
*O sacrament divine,*
*All praise and all thanksgiving,*
*Be every moment thine!*

Let us proclaim this mystery of faith!

MOST REVEREND TIMOTHY M. DOLAN
ARCHBISHOP OF MILWAUKEE
JULY 2004

*An Irish bishop recited the following ditty during a sermon: "Paddy Murphy went to Mass, and never missed a Sunday. But Paddy Murphy went to hell, for what he did on Monday."*

*There's an important lesson in this ditty: that our lives must be in conformity with our worship. The name* Mass *comes from the Latin dismissal formula Ite, Missa est.*

The Eucharist, the *Catechism of the Catholic Church* adds, is called "*Holy Mass (Missa),* because the liturgy in which the mystery of salvation is accomplished concludes with the sending forth *(missio)* of the faithful, so that they may fulfill God's will in their daily lives" (*CCC* 1332).

"Go in peace to love and serve the Lord." We leave the church building after Mass to go and live the Mass. This is "Eucharistic Spirituality."

# Living the Mass

The word *spirituality* has many meanings. To understand its most profound sense, however, we should begin with the Mass as it is described in this passage from the *Catechism*:

> The Eucharist is "the source and summit of the Christian life" (Lumen Gentium). "The other sacraments, and indeed all ecclesiastical ministries and works of the apostolate, are bound up with the Eucharist and are oriented toward it. For in the blessed Eucharist is contained the whole spiritual good of the Church, namely Christ himself, our Pasch" (Presbyterorum ordinis, 5) (CCC 1324).

Spirituality is the spiritual life, that is, living in God, with God, and for God. Spirituality begins with the realization that our world of material things does not mark out the boundaries of our existence. The "really real," with no beginning or end, is God, who is being itself: "I AM WHO I AM" (Ex 3:14). To the extent that we share in God's life and are united to the love of Father, Son, and Holy Spirit, our life expands beyond the limits of space and time. It shakes off the shackles imposed by weakness or age. It reaches to horizons that never end because they shine with God's everlasting light.

Some humans tend to live as if physical matter were the only reality. This misconception is reinforced by advertising which, for obvious reasons, focuses on what can be bought and sold. The material world is real, and it is good. It bears the stamp of divine approval. "God saw everything that he had made, and indeed, it was very good" (Gen 1:31). But it is limited. The goodness of material things and of human bodily existence flows from its source, unlimited Goodness, almighty God. Matter is created by the divine wisdom and energy which gave it being. After all, as Einstein demonstrated, $E = mc^2$!

True spirituality recognizes God's presence in all creation. Created things are not God, of course, but they point to God as their maker and sustainer: "The heavens are telling the glory of God" (Ps 19:1a). Sin placed a veil between humanity and God's glory, as the story of creation shows so dramatically in the attempt of Adam and Eve to hide from God (see Gen 3:8). But Jesus Christ removed that veil when he came into our world. At his birth, the glory of the Lord shone upon the humblest of people (see Lk 2:9). When lowly shepherds looked upon Jesus, they saw "the glory of God in the face of Jesus Christ" (2 Cor 4:6). Catholic spirituality, then, *is* Jesus Christ.

# Living Is Christ

Saint Paul wrote, "For to me, living is Christ..." (Phil 1:21). To be a Catholic, to live a Catholic spiritual life, is to know Christ as Son of God and as our Lord and Savior. The *Catechism* says,

> *At the heart of catechesis we find, in essence, a Person, the Person of Jesus of Nazareth, the only Son from the Father...who suffered and died for us and who now, after rising, is living with us forever."* To catechize is *"to reveal in the Person of Christ the whole of God's eternal design reaching fulfillment in that Person. It is to seek to understand the meaning of Christ's actions and words and of the signs worked by him."* Catechesis aims at putting *"people...in communion ...with Jesus Christ: only he can lead us to the love of the Father in the Spirit and make us share in the life of the Holy Trinity"* (CCC 426, *quoting* Catechesi tradendae, 5).

How does the Mass fit into this statement? Jesus alone can bestow true spirituality by granting us a share in the life of the Holy Trinity. God comes to us in Jesus Christ. And Jesus comes to us first and foremost in the Mass.

God "condenses" divinity in Jesus to reveal the incredible extent of divine love in the heart of God. Then Jesus "condenses" the power of his life, death, and Resurrection in the Mass; he "condenses" his humanity and divinity in the Eucharist. Through the Mass and in holy Communion, we meet God!

That is why the Eucharist is the "source and summit of the Christian life," for "in the blessed Eucharist is contained…Christ himself." We who are Catholic must be sure of this. Our beliefs, sacraments, apostolic works, ministries, lives, and spirituality are centered in Christ.

Sadly, some Catholics fail to realize this point. A few years ago Miriam told me that she never knew Jesus while she was a Catholic. The day after Pope John Paul II visited Saint Louis, a caller to a radio talk show announced that he didn't know Jesus personally until he left Catholicism. Obviously, such people could not have understood their Catholic Faith or believed what the Church teaches. They could not have recognized Christ's Real Presence in the Eucharist and in his Church. But how could they miss it?

When I asked this question during a discussion at a religious education convention, one teacher said she thought the reason might be that "Catholicism has so many riches to present that we forget to relate them to Jesus." But the *Catechism* tells us: "In catechesis 'Christ, the Incarnate Word and Son of God...is taught—everything else is taught with reference to him'" (*CCC* 427, quoting *Catechesi tradendae*, 5). We must relate all the riches of our faith to Jesus, find Jesus in them, and bring to the world these riches—above all—the riches of the Eucharist.

# "Either/Or, Both/And"

If some Catholics fail to find Jesus in the Catholic Church, those outside the Church who criticize Catholicism surely do not understand how Jesus makes himself available. After Pope John Paul II celebrated Mass at the America's Center in Saint Louis on January 27, 1999, those of us who attended were approached by people handing out anti-Catholic brochures attacking various aspects of Catholic belief. One pamphlet read: "Friend, you can RIGHT NOW be saved and KNOW that you have ETERNAL LIFE, if you will put your complete faith in Jesus Christ, and stop relying on yourself, church, sacraments, or anything else to save or help save you. Jesus is the Savior. Do you believe he can save you, or don't you?"

Those who compose such anti-Catholic literature separate Christ from the Church he founded and deny his teachings. The Church did not create the sacraments. Jesus did. It was Jesus who said, "This is my Body" and "If you forgive the sins of others, they are forgiven."

Unfortunately, those who attack Catholicism often rely on false "either-or" dilemmas. "Do you believe in Jesus, *or* do you believe in his Church and sacraments?" We Catholics believe that Christianity is a matter not of "either-or" but of "both-and." We believe in Jesus Christ *and* in his Church and sacraments. It is through the Church and sacraments that Jesus comes to us today. Jesus is not only a historical figure. Jesus is not just up in the sky. He's right here with us, through the Church and sacraments which make his presence both visible and tangible.

Catholicism is a sacramental Church. We believe that God the Son became one of us so that he might be a visible sign (*sacrament*) of God's presence. Each of the seven sacraments given us by Jesus are the visible signs through which he continues to act in our midst. The Eucharist *is* Jesus, and therefore the source and summit of sacramental life, as the *Catechism* states: "The other sacraments…are bound up with the Eucharist and are oriented toward it" (*CCC* 1324, quoting *Presbyterorum ordinis*, 5).

The more we know about the Eucharist, the more we will be brought to Jesus. After all, it is Jesus who leads us in prayer at Mass, who proclaims the Scriptures to us, and who makes his dwelling in our hearts at holy Communion. And it is Jesus whom we can proclaim to those who, perhaps out of misguided zeal, ask questions such as, "Have you accepted Jesus as your savior?" "Are you saved?" Our response to the first question might be, "Yes, I accept Jesus into my heart each time I receive him in holy Communion. He abides in me and I abide in him" (see Jn 6:56). Our answer to the second: "Jesus died for my salvation, and he makes the power of his death and Resurrection present to me at every Mass. I set all my hope on the grace that Jesus brings (see 1 Pet 1:13). Salvation is my life's journey."

When confronted by such questions, we should always explain our reason for hope, as Scripture says, "with gentleness and reverence" (1 Pet 3:16), and even with a sense of humor. Jerry was playing tennis when he fell backward on the concrete court, fracturing his skull in three places. His friends called 911, and a helicopter quickly landed nearby. A paramedic stabilized him and kept him alive while he was flown to a hospital. Later Jerry met the paramedic. He was Hispanic, and his name was Jesus. Jerry smiles and says, "I feel blessed to have been saved by Jesus!"

We have all been saved by Jesus in the sense that through his life, death, and Resurrection, Jesus has done everything necessary to bring us to heaven. But we must, in our turn, freely stay united to Jesus by faith and good works (see Jas 2:26; Eph 2:10). Salvation *is* our life's journey!

# Father, Son, and Holy Spirit

If we meet Jesus at every Mass and realize how he is the heart and center of our Catholic faith, we cannot help but be led into a deeper relationship with the Father and Holy Spirit as well. In his Last Supper discourse (see Jn 13–17), Jesus promised that he, the Father, and the Holy Spirit would live in us. Jesus wanted us to see the Mass as a means of joining ourselves to the life and love of the Trinity.

For we live in a Trinitarian world. From all eternity the Father knows himself with a knowledge so perfect that it is a person, the Son. The Father and Son love each other with a love so perfect that it is a person, the Holy Spirit. From this knowledge and love flow all that exists, including ourselves. Since we have been made by God, who is perfect knowledge and love, we hunger for perfect truth and love. That hunger will be satisfied only to the extent that we know and love God as Father, Son, and Holy Spirit. Mass is the best opportunity this side of heaven to strengthen our relationship with Father, Son, and Spirit.

Every Mass brings us into contact with the Trinity. As Mass begins, we make the Sign of the Cross. As Mass ends, Father, Son, and Holy Spirit bless us. During Mass, we pray to the Father, through Jesus Christ our Lord, in the unity of the Holy Spirit. We profess our Faith in Father, Son, and Holy Spirit. At Mass, Jesus offers a perfect sacrifice of love to the Father, and we are privileged to join our own love to his. The Holy Spirit helps us make our offering and pray as we ought. When we receive Jesus in holy Communion, we receive also the Father and Holy Spirit, who are one with him.

Each time we leave Mass, going "in peace to love and serve the Lord," Jesus invites us to live a Trinitarian spirituality. In my book *The Search for Happiness*, I explain an approach to this spirituality built around the Lord's Prayer, the beatitudes, and the fruits of the Holy Spirit. Here I would like to suggest a three-minute prayer to help anyone stay in touch with the Trinity. In the first minute, think about the greatest blessing you've received in the past twenty-four hours and thank God the Father for that blessing. In the second, consider your most significant failing in the past twenty-four hours and ask Jesus to forgive you. In the third, look ahead to the greatest challenge that faces you in the next twenty-four hours and ask the Holy Spirit to be your helper and guide as you accept that challenge. Use this prayer often, and you'll be more conscious of the reality that we are "the temple of the living God" (2 Cor 6:16).

# Living the Paschal Mystery

The Mass commemorates and makes present the Paschal Mystery, Christ's work of redemption brought about primarily by his passion, death, Resurrection, and Ascension (*CCC* 1067). Christ's Passover from death to life, his passage from death on the cross to glory at the Father's right hand, is presented at every Mass so that we might praise and thank God for this great act of love. The Paschal Mystery is also a pattern for us. With Christ, we conquer death and rise to new life. "Dying you destroyed our death. Rising you restored our life." In Christ our greatest fears are overcome as death is defeated and we learn to live in the freedom of God's children.

The Paschal Mystery shines light into every darkness. There is a kind of death in the frustration of failure, the loss of a job, conflict in the family, the departure of a friend, the onset of illness, the pain of depression, the betrayal of a trust. Such deaths weigh us down and drain us of energy and hope.

To these deaths the Paschal Mystery brings resurrection. At Calvary, Christ's mission seemed to have failed utterly. His disciples despaired. But Easter bestowed life where there had been death. Jesus brings hope into every situation. He is, as he declared at the Last Supper, "the way, and the truth, and the life" (Jn 14:6a).

His death and Resurrection are the *way* through every hard journey we face. His teaching in Scripture, proclaimed at every Mass, is the *truth* that guides us in times of confusion and failure. His Real Presence in holy Communion is the *life* that lifts us from any grave of discouragement or fear.

As Jesus walked with the two disciples on the way to Emmaus (see Lk 24), so he wants to walk with us every day. We need not leave him in church! As Jesus speaks to us in the readings at Mass, so he wants to speak to us each time we read the Bible. The Scriptures are not confined to the pulpit! As Jesus gives us his life in holy Communion, so he desires to abide in us always, allowing the life of his grace to flow through our veins. We the branches are not separated from Christ the Vine when we exit Mass for home!

# The Liturgical Year

People like to celebrate birthdays and anniversaries. We have holidays to recall milestones in our nation's history. Such celebrations help us remember the past. They bring joy and festivity. They refresh and invigorate us for the routine of everyday existence. The liturgical year is the Church's way of celebrating and reliving the great events of salvation. Each year follows a pattern, and the readings and prayers for Mass have been organized to bring joy and festivity, refreshment and new vigor to the ever-changing seasons of life.

The liturgical year begins with Advent, four weeks of preparation for Christmas. On December 25 we observe the birthday of Christ and reflect on the Incarnation. After Christmas, other feasts extend the celebration: Holy Family Sunday, the Solemnity of Mary the Mother of God (New Year's Day), Epiphany, and the Baptism of the Lord.

There follows a period of Ordinary Time, the

length of which depends on the date of Easter. The Lenten preparation for Easter begins on Ash Wednesday when we are marked with ashes, signaling our desire to make the Paschal Mystery the pattern of our existence. As catechumens make final preparations for baptism, all Catholics are challenged to die to sin and rise to new life. Lent ends at the sacred triduum, three days which recall the events of the first Holy Thursday, Good Friday, and Holy Saturday. We celebrate the Resurrection with the Easter Vigil and the Masses of Easter, the greatest feast of the Church year. Easter season continues through the Feast of the Ascension and ends on Pentecost Sunday.

Ordinary Time resumes the day after Pentecost, but the next two Sundays commemorate the Trinity and the Body and Blood of Christ. Ordinary Time continues through the last Sunday of the liturgical year, the Solemnity of Christ the King, after which the First Sunday of Advent starts the cycle again.

Christ is free of the limits of space and time and relives with us the events of his life through the liturgical year. Through Scripture readings appropriate to the events being celebrated, God speaks to us. We respond by participating in the liturgy and so are joined to the birth, life, dying, and rising of Jesus as once again he walks the pathways of our world.

Most major liturgical observances occur on Sunday, but there are also special feasts in the liturgical year called holy days of obligation. In the United States, we observe the following holy days: Christmas on the twenty-fifth of December; the Solemnity of Mary the Mother of God on the first of January; Ascension (now usually celebrated on the Seventh Sunday of Easter); Mary's Assumption on the fifteenth of August; All Saints' Day on the first of November; and the Immaculate Conception on the eighth of December.

Throughout the liturgical year, the Catholic Church keeps feast days in honor of Mary and the saints. As we remember their lives in special prayers at Mass and ask them to pray for us, we heed the biblical command "Remember your leaders, those who spoke the word of God to you; consider the outcome of their way of life, and imitate their faith" (Heb 13:7). Commemorating the saints also proclaims the centrality of Christ, for their lives demonstrate the power of his life, death, and Resurrection shared with humanity. The saints show the joy and beauty of putting Jesus first and letting his Paschal Mystery be the pattern for our lives.

# The Other Sacraments

"The other sacraments...are bound up with the Eucharist and are oriented toward it" (*CCC* 1324). It is Jesus who is present in the Eucharist, and it is Jesus who speaks and acts through all the sacraments. The Mass makes present the Paschal Mystery of Jesus' life, death, Resurrection, and Ascension, and the other sacraments also give us a share in this Mystery. The Church professes belief in these realities and in the interconnection between the Mass and sacraments in many ways. Here we will note how the celebration of the Eucharist is linked to that of the other sacraments.

*Baptism,* which first joins us to Christ in his dying and rising, is most dramatically united to the Eucharist in the great Easter Vigil, which welcome new members into the Church. As the congregation is drawn from the darkness of night into the light of Christ, the baptized step from the darkness of sin into the brightness of God's grace. The receive an outpouring of the Holy Spirit in confirmation, then are nourished with the Body and Blood of Jesus.

*Ritual Masses* for confirmation, holy orders, matrimony, and the anointing of the sick highlight the eucharistic presence and power of Jesus. In confirmation, he pours out the Holy Spirit, a gift made possible by his passion, death, and Resurrection (see Jn 16:7). In holy orders, Jesus says to the newly ordained what he said to the apostles at the Last Supper: "Do this in memory of me." In matrimony, Jesus, living in the bride and groom, binds them together in their exchange of vows and in their acceptance of his Body and Blood; their love then becomes a sign of his love for the Church (see Eph 5:32). In the anointing of the sick, Jesus offers the healing power of the love he demonstrated by his death, and he gives comfort and hope as those anointed receive him in Communion.

*The penitential rite* at Mass reminds us that we are sinners in need of God's forgiveness. It assures us, as we pray "Lord, have mercy," that the same Jesus who gathers us together at the Eucharist is ever present in the sacrament of penance to forgive our sins.

Finally, when life on this earth has ended for believers, *the funeral Mass* proclaims that those who die with Christ rise with him to eternal life. Jesus speaks words of consolation to the bereaved in the Scripture readings. He unites them to their loved one in the Eucharistic Prayer. He promises them at Communion that those who eat this bread will live forever (see Jn 6:58).

From birth until death, from baptism, through the anointing of the sick, and funeral Mass, we are reassured by eucharistic celebrations that Jesus continues to share with us the love and grace he lavished upon the apostles at the Last Supper. Indeed "the other sacraments…are bound up with the Eucharist and are oriented toward it."

# Eucharistic Devotions

In every parish I've served as a priest, I have been blessed by the dedication of people who attend daily Mass. Physicians, business owners, teachers, and laborers rise early to worship at Mass before dawn. Home-schooling moms bring their children to the Eucharist before starting classes. Retirees begin their day with prayer and the Mass. Some folks cannot come every day but attend whenever possible. Such individuals radiate faith in Jesus and love of others by the sacrifices they make in uniting themselves to the sacrifice of the Mass. They have inspired me, and they have been avenues of God's grace for countless others.

Daily Mass is *the* most powerful way to live a eucharistic spirituality. The Sunday Mass, as we have seen, has a special place in the Church's liturgy. It is the Lord's day. But every day belongs to God, and there is no better way to let Jesus touch our lives than union with him at daily Mass.

However, it is not possible for many people to attend Mass every day. For such individuals there are other eucharistic devotions to help them stay close to Jesus. Christ's Real Presence in the Eucharist remains after Mass is over. For this reason, the Catholic Church preserves the Blessed Sacrament in tabernacles throughout the world to make Communion available to the sick and to allow the faithful to adore Christ in the Eucharist.

The Church highly recommends public and private devotion to the holy Eucharist outside Mass. An important public devotion is exposition of the Blessed Sacrament with Benediction, an act of liturgical worship. The consecrated host is placed on the altar in a monstrance (a sacred vessel in which the host may be seen). Scriptures are read, prayers are said, hymns are sung, and time is devoted to silent prayer. Adoration is expressed with incense. Then the congregation is blessed with the Holy Sacrament, and the service concludes with prayers and a hymn. This devotion clearly demonstrates our Catholic belief in Christ's Eucharistic Presence, and it nourishes and strengthens that belief.

Pope John Paul II has emphasized the value of eucharistic adoration, the practice of spending time with Jesus in the Blessed Sacrament. In his encyclical letter *Ecclesia De Eucharistia*, he pointed out both the importance of this devotion and its relationship to the Mass:

> *The worship of the Eucharist outside of the Mass is of inestimable value for the life of the Church. This worship is strictly linked to the celebration of the Eucharistic Sacrifice. The presence of Christ under the sacred species reserved after Mass—a presence which lasts as long as the species of bread and of wine remain—derives from the celebration of the sacrifice and is directed towards communion, both sacramental and spiritual (25).*

Many Catholic parishes have instituted the practice of perpetual adoration, where members of the faithful maintain a constant presence before the Blessed Sacrament exposed on the altar. Other parishes set aside a day or two each week for adoration.

From such eucharistic adoration flows many benefits, including vocations to the priesthood and religious life, new appreciation of the sacrament of matrimony, and greater concern for charity and justice.

Whether the Blessed Sacrament is exposed or not, Jesus remains available to us in every Catholic church. An hour in the presence of Jesus has been a source of grace for many. Bishop Fulton Sheen, in his retreat talks, strongly recommended the practice of spending an hour every day in the presence of the Blessed Sacrament. This hour has been for me one of the greatest blessings of my priesthood. I heartily recommend it to all. If you can't fit in an hour every day, try an hour a week. It will make the rest of your week more pleasant and productive.

What might we do during this hour of prayer? First, there should be time to enjoy being with Jesus as did Andrew and another apostle who met Jesus and spent a day visiting with him (Jn 1:35–42). They must have talked about their families, their work, and what was happening in their lives. So, too, can we. We can receive, as the pope suggests, "spiritual communion"—inviting Jesus to live in our heart even when we cannot receive him sacramentally. We may pray the rosary, paying special attention to how the mysteries relate to the Eucharist, to the presence of Jesus, to his teaching, and to the Paschal Mystery of his passion, death, Resurrection, and Ascension. We should reflect upon Scripture, especially those passages used at the Sunday Masses, another excellent way to relate our time of adoration to the Mass. Some individuals like to read from a good Catholic book, pausing to talk to Jesus about thoughts that touch their hearts. Those who get into the habit of making an hour of adoration in the presence of Jesus find that the time goes by all too quickly, just as it does in the presence of any good friend!

As we develop our awareness of Christ's Real Presence in all the tabernacles of the world, we learn to notice Catholic churches and to say a prayer to Jesus as we walk or drive past his home. We pray a "morning offering" early in the day, giving to the Father our hopes, plans, and efforts in union with the offering of Jesus in Masses being celebrated at that moment. We make a spiritual Communion anytime or anywhere, remembering Jesus' words: "Listen! I am standing at the door, knocking; if you hear my voice and open the door, I will come in to you and eat with you, and you with me" (Rev 3:20).

Pope John Paul II, in his apostolic letter *Dies Domini*, refers to televised Masses as a means of joining oneself to the Eucharist. Televised Masses do not take the place of Sunday Mass, but as the pope notes,

> *...for those who cannot take part in the Eucharist and who are therefore excused from the obligation, radio and television are a precious help, especially if accompanied by the generous service of extraordinary ministers who bring the Eucharist to the sick, also bringing them the greeting and solidarity of the whole community. Sunday Mass thus produces rich fruits for these Christians too, and they are truly enabled to experience Sunday as "the Lord's Day" and "the Church's day"* (54).

Televised Masses allow anyone to grow in love o the Eucharist as they provide a pattern for praye and reflection. Special Masses, such as those celebrated by the Holy Father and shown worldwide, help us appreciate the power of the Eucharist to touch all people and to draw us together in Christ.

The pope's mention of extraordinary ministers who bring Communion to the sick highlights another element of eucharistic spirituality that is a great blessing for ministers and for the homebound. It is a blessing to hold Jesus close to one's heart, to talk with him on the way, to share the grace of his presence with those who otherwise could not receive him. It is a blessing for the sick and elderly to have Jesus enter their residence, to light up their lives, to be one with them in their suffering, to lessen their pain, and to assure them that he will be with them forever.

# The Eucharist
# and Loving Service

At the Last Supper, Jesus forged an unbreakable bond between works of charity and the Eucharist. He washed the feet of the apostles, then said, "For I have set you an example, that you also should do as I have done to you" (Jn 13:15). Later that evening, Jesus remarked, "This is my commandment, that you love one another as I have loved you" (Jn 15:12).

From New Testament times, followers of Jesus have attended to his words and example. In the Acts of the Apostles, the believers "devoted themselves to the apostles' teaching and fellowship, to the breaking of bread and the prayers" (Acts 2:42). The same ones who met for the breaking of the bread "would sell their possessions and goods and distribute the proceeds to all, as any had need" (Acts 2:45).

Saint Paul, writing to the Corinthians about a collection for the poor in Jerusalem, linked this work of charity to the Sunday Eucharist, repeating directions he had given also to the churches of Galatia. "On the first day of every week, each of you is to put aside and save whatever extra you earn…" (1 Cor 16:2). Earlier in his letter, because the Corinthians had neglected the bond between the Eucharist and concern for the poor, Paul sternly rebuked them: "When you come together, it is not really to eat the Lord's supper. For when the time comes to eat, each of you goes ahead with your own supper, and one goes hungry and another becomes drunk. What! Do you not have homes to eat and drink in? Or do you show contempt for the church of God and humiliate those who have nothing?" (1 Cor 11:20–22).

Saint Justin Martyr demonstrates that the next generation of Christians learned the lessons taught by Paul. After describing the Sunday celebration of the Eucharist, he states,

*And they who are well to do, and willing, give what each thinks fit; and what is collected is deposited with the president, who helps the orphans and widows and those who, through sickness or any other cause, are in want, and those who are*

*in bonds and the strangers sojourning among us,*
*and in a word takes care of all who are in need*
(First Apology, *Chapter 67, available at*
*www.catholic-forum.com/saints/stj29002.htm*).

Pope John Paul II affirms that the Sunday Eucharist commits Catholics to the works of charity, mercy, and apostolic outreach:

*From the Sunday Mass there flows a tide of charity destined to spread into the whole life of the faithful.... They look around to find people who may need their help. It may be that in their neighborhood or among those they know there are sick people, elderly people, children or immigrants who precisely on Sundays feel more keenly their isolation, needs and suffering.... Inviting to a meal people who are alone, visiting the sick, providing food for needy families, spending a few hours in voluntary work and acts of solidarity: these would certainly be ways of bringing into people's lives the love of Christ received at the Eucharistic table* (Dies Domini, *72*).

In his encyclical letter *Ecclesia de Eucharistia*, the pope speaks of how the Mass gives hope and spurs us on to address the urgent needs of our time, to work for peace, justice, solidarity, and respect for human life. Inherent in the Eucharist is a "commitment to transforming the world in accordance with the Gospel" (#20). Jesus himself teaches that our eternal salvation depends on personal efforts to serve him in others. "Come, you that are blessed by my Father, inherit the kingdom prepared for you from the foundation of the world; for I was hungry and you gave me food, I was thirsty and you gave me something to drink, I was a stranger and you welcomed me" (Mt 25:34–35). The *Catechism of the Catholic Church* says simply, "The Eucharist commits us to the poor" (*CCC* 1397).

# Charity Begins at Home

At the Last Supper, Jesus washed the feet of his apostles, who were his chosen family. Charity does begin at home, and our works of charity and justice should start among those with whom we live. It is often easier to show kindness and patience to strangers than to family members, whose failings are obvious and ever present.

It can be easier to dream of saving the world than to love the ones you're with. At times we all feel like the little boy who said, "I know Jesus loves everyone, but he never met my sister." Well, Jesus' apostles were far from perfect, and he loved them anyway. We, too, must love our family members anyway, striving to focus on their good points and to forgive their weaknesses.

At Mass we listen to God's Word to learn how to love. We are joined to the love and sacrificial giving of Jesus. We receive him in holy Communion. We must bring him home with us. I often ask children,

"If Jesus would disguise himself as you, and then went home instead of you, would your family notice a difference?" Their response is always in the affirmative, and always with a smile. Then I'll suggest: "Why don't you pretend you are Jesus. Try to think, talk, and act like him. Surprise your family!"

This would be good advice for any of us. If we think like Jesus, we will look for the best in others. We will subdue thoughts of anger and feelings of resentment. We will consider the needs of others before our own. If we speak like Jesus, we will use words of encouragement rather than of criticism, words of forgiveness rather than of hostility, words of respect rather than of sarcasm, words of gratitude rather than of complaint. If we act like Jesus, we will express love in practical ways, performing everyday tasks for others when no one but God will notice, being polite, considerate, and thoughtful. The sacramental presence of Jesus ceases when the sacramental species no longer exist. But Jesus continues to live in us when our thoughts, words, and deeds mirror his love and goodness.

*Receiving the Bread of Life, the disciples of Christ ready themselves to undertake with the strength of the Risen Lord and his Spirit the tasks which await them in their ordinary life. For the faithful who have understood the meaning of what they have done, the eucharistic celebration does not stop at the church door. Like the first witnesses of the Resurrection, Christians who gather each Sunday to experience and proclaim the presence of the Risen Lord are called to evangelize and bear witness in their daily lives (John Paul II, Dies Domini, 45).*

# What They Did on Monday

The Eucharist is surely "the source and summit of the Christian life." Eucharistic spirituality is knowing Jesus Christ as our way, truth, and life. It is entering, through Jesus, into the life of the Trinity. It is living the Paschal Mystery, knowing that Jesus will transform our suffering and death into resurrection and new life. It is walking with Jesus through the liturgical year, allowing the events of his life to be a pattern for ours. It is union with Jesus through prayer, eucharistic adoration, and attentiveness to his presence. It is serving the cause of justice and charity. It is taking Jesus home as we "go in peace to love and serve the Lord."

Living a eucharistic spirituality will make it possible for us one day to hear the words of a new ditty:

*"These Catholics went to Mass and never missed a Sunday. And these Catholics went to HEAVEN for what they did on Monday!"*

# Questions for
# Discussion and Reflection

Can you give your own definition of spirituality? Of Christian spirituality? Is it possible to live a truly Christian spirituality without being religious, without participating in religious rites?

When asked why he goes to daily Mass and what it has meant to him, Jim responded: "Going to daily Mass helps me to remember to put God first in my life, to give God glory, and to get to know God better. I have a sense of peace in my life even in the midst of very difficult situations. Mass has also helped lead me back to frequent confession, which has also been an incredible blessing. Daily Mass has strengthened my family life." If you attend daily Mass, what does it mean to you? If not, what could it mean for you if you did?

There are many suggestions in this pamphlet for living a eucharistic spirituality. First, scan the main headings of this pamphlet. Then consider the following: What additional aspects of eucharistic spirituality do you think should be discussed within these headings? What other headings do you think should be added? Are there approaches to spirituality in this pamphlet with which you disagree? Why? (Any criticisms, comments, or suggestions may be sent to the author at frlukecm@cs.com.)

# Activities

Christian spirituality is the spiritual life, living in God, with God, and for God, with Jesus as our guide and model. It includes much more than can be included in this pamphlet. For an explanation of how living in Christ finds expression in Catholic moral teaching, see Chapter Fourteen of my book *"We Believe..." A Survey of the Catholic Faith* (Liguori Publications, 1995). As already noted, *The Search for Happiness* (Liguori, 2002) offers an outline for living a Trinitarian spirituality built on the Lord's Prayer, the beatitudes, and the fruits of the Holy Spirit. *The Privilege of Being Catholic* (Liguori, 1993) shows that our Catholic Faith and spirituality are sacramental in nature because Jesus himself is a visible, sacramental sign of God's reality and presence. And remember that any Catholic spirituality must include the Eucharist precisely because, as the *Catechism of the Catholic Church* states, it is "the source and summit of the Christian life."

Mary stood by the cross of Jesus and shared his suffering. She can help us draw strength from her crucified Son at every Mass and in every place. A Marian devotion I've found very helpful is to replace feelings of anger and frustration with a Hail Mary for those who test my patience. On some days I say a lot of Hail Marys! But I find that the prayers bring far more peace and happiness than giving in to hostile emotions. I try to remember that Mary, standing at the cross, endured more misunderstanding and hatred in three hours than I will in a lifetime. Mary thereby helps me learn how to live the Mass each day. Try this way of praying and she will help you, too.

# Bibliography

*Catechism of the Catholic Church*. Second Edition. United States Catholic Conference, 1997.

*General Instruction of the Roman Missal*. United States Catholic Conference, 2003.

Lukefahr, Oscar. *The Privilege of Being Catholic*. Liguori, Mo.: Liguori Publications, 1993.

_____. *The Search for Happiness*. Liguori, Mo.: Liguori Publications, 2002.

_____. *"We Believe…" A Survey of the Catholic Faith*. Second Edition. Liguori, Mo.: Liguori Publications, 1995.

_____. *We Worship: A Guide to the Catholic Mass*. Liguori, Mo.: Liguori Publications, 2004.

*New Revised Standard Version of the Bible: Catholic Edition*. Nashville, Tenn.: Catholic Bible Press, 1993.